10/12

 W9-CBR-417

KILLER BEARS

Alex Woolf

ARCTURUS

This edition first published in 2011 by Arcturus Publishing

Distributed by Black Rabbit Books
P.O. Box 3263
Mankato
Minnesota MN 56002

Copyright © 2011 Arcturus Publishing Limited

Printed in China

Library of Congress Cataloging-in-Publication Data

Woolf, Alex, 1964-
 Killer bears / Alex Woolf.
    p. cm. -- (Animal attack)
 Includes index.
 ISBN 978-1-84837-945-9 (library binding)
1. Bears--Juvenile literature. 2. Dangerous animals--Juvenile literature. I. Title.
 QL737.C27W669 2012
 599.78--dc22
                         2011006624

The right of Alex Woolf to be identified as the author of this work has been asserted by him in accordance with the
Copyright, Designs and Patents Act 1988.

Series concept: Alex Woolf
Editor and picture researcher: Alex Woolf
Designer: Ian Winton
Cover designer: Peter Ridley

Picture credits
Corbis: cover (Renee Lynn), 4 (Galen Rowell), 8 (Steven Kazlowski/Science Faction), 14 (Radius Images), 17
(DiMaggio/Kalish), 20 *top* (Kennan Ward), 23 (Jay Ryser/First Light), 25 *top* (Jenny E. Ross).
Dantheman9758: 28 *top*.
The Field Museum: 28 *bottom* (Beth Sanzenbacher).
Krause, Hans: 29.
Shutterstock: 5 *top* (Fotomicar), 5 *bottom* (Dennis Donohue), 6 (Florian Andronache), 7 *top* (Antoni Murcia), 7
bottom (Arto Hakola), 9 (Ronnie Howard), 10 (Mighty Sequoia Studio), 11 (Antoni Murcia),
12 (Graham Bloomfield), 15 (jadimages), 16 *top* (Jerry Sharp), 16 *bottom* (Scott Kapich), 18 (Bonnie Fink), 19 (Darla
Hallmark), 20 *bottom* (Tyler Olson), 21 (Gail Johnson), 22 (saranvaid), 24 (Lisa F. Young),
25 *bottom* (tonobalaguerf), 26 (Alistair Michael Thomas), 27 (Eric Gevaert).

Every attempt has been made to clear copyright. Should there be any inadvertent omission, please apply to the
publisher for rectification.

Supplier 03, Date 0411, Print Run 1041
SL001706US

Contents

The Bear Facts

A full-throated bear roar—one of nature's more awesome sights and sounds!

Despite their cuddly image, bears are among the most terrifying predators on the planet. Their huge size and strength combined with sharp teeth and claws make them formidable hunters.

To keep up their strength, bears must eat huge quantities—and not just the animals and fish they kill. They also eat fruit, plants, seeds, eggs, insects, and carrion.

SNACK ON THIS!

Winnie the Pooh's love of honey is based on fact! To satisfy their sweet tooth, bears use their strong paws to rip open beehives and eat all the honey. Their thick fur protects them from stings.

Bears in brief

- **Prey:** Small mammals, fish, insects
- **Tools:** Strength, speed, sense of smell, sharp teeth, and claws
- **Methods:** Search and stalk, ambush, chase, scavenge

Most bears have poor eyesight and hearing. But they make up for this with a powerful sense of smell, which they use to guide them to their food.

(Above) A brown bear snacks on a carrot.

(Left) Although they usually move slowly, bears can run very fast—up to 35 miles per hour—which is useful when chasing prey.

5

Brown Bear

The brown bear is the most well known of all bear species. It is found in many different parts of the world, especially in isolated mountain regions and dense forests.

Brown bears are omnivores—they like all kinds of food, especially fish, birds, mammals, carrion, roots, berries, and herbs.

You can spot a brown bear from its shoulder hump—a large mass of muscle that helps it dig up roots, move rocks, and tear apart logs to find food.

SNACK ON THIS!

Brown bears rise onto their hind legs and often bite or hold the victim's lower jaw to avoid being bitten themselves. They occasionally attack humans.

Brown bear facts

- **Where?** North America, Europe, and Asia
- **How heavy?** 300-900 lb.
- **How big?** Up to 10 ft. tall

Brown bear cubs face many dangers from predators—including some adult male bears!

The bigger bears hunt large mammals such as moose and caribou. The largest brown bears of all live in coastal areas where they feed on protein-rich salmon.

Brown bears often steal the kills of other predators, such as wolves. This bear is using its size and strength to scare the wolf away.

Grizzly Bear

The grizzly is a type of brown bear and one of the most dangerous animals in North America. A single blow from its mighty paw can break the neck or back of a moose.

The bear gets its name because its brown fur is tipped with silver-gray, making it look grizzled.

The grizzly's rear legs are strong enough to support its entire weight. Most animals walk on tiptoes, but the grizzly walks on the soles of its feet—just like a human.

SNACK ON THIS!

Grizzlies have a fantastic sense of smell. Some scientists say a grizzly can smell carrion from 18 miles away.

During the summer and autumn, the grizzly may eat up to 80–90 pounds of food per day—the equivalent of about 300 hamburgers! It builds up a layer of extra fat to allow it to survive the winter, when it may eat nothing for months.

Grizzlies often fight each other over food and territory.

Grizzly bear facts

- **How heavy?** 330-500 lb.
- **How big?** Around 8 ft. tall
- **Where?** The Rockies of North America, from Alaska to Colorado.

More About Grizzlies

Grizzlies are among the most aggressive bears in the world, and one of the most likely to attack humans.

They are at their most dangerous when cornered or wounded. A female defending her cubs is also likely to be aggressive. However, few grizzlies actively hunt humans. By far their favorite food is fish.

A mother bear teaches her cubs how to catch fish.

More grizzly facts

- **How fast?** Up to 40 mph
- **Lifespan:** Around 25 years in the wild
- **Favorite veggie snacks:** Plants, berries, grass, leaves, roots

Like most bears, grizzlies live and hunt alone. However, once a year, during the summer, when the streams fill with salmon, grizzlies come together to fish.

Grizzlies use different fishing methods, depending on how their mothers taught them. Some stand still in the water and wait for a fish to jump out. Then they catch it in their jaws. Others use their paws to swat the fish out of the water and onto the shore.

SNACK ON THIS!

Some grizzlies swim underwater to find salmon, or stun the fish by bellyflopping on top of them!

11

Kodiak Bear

The kodiak bear shares with the polar bear the status of world's largest land predator. Standing ten feet tall on its hind legs, this enormous beast would be as tall as the high diving board at many swimming pools.

Two kodiaks enjoy a play fight. Watch it with those teeth!

It is found on the islands of the Kodiak Archipelago in south-western Alaska. This is a salmon spawning ground, offering the kodiaks plentiful quantitles of their favorite food.

SNACK ON THIS!

A female kodiak can catch up to 15 salmon an hour to feed herself and her cubs.

The kodiak diet of high-protein, fatty salmon is the main reason for their huge size.

Kodiaks are not just big, they're also bright, with an intelligence estimated at somewhere between that of a dog and an ape.

CHEW ON THAT!

The oldest kodiak bear ever found in the wild was 35 years old.

They have developed a complex language of noises and body movements and have recognizable personalities. They also have much better eyesight and hearing than the average bear.

A kodiak chomps a breakfast treat.

13

American black bear

The American black bear lives in the mountainous or heavily wooded areas of Canada, the United States and Mexico. They are called black bears, but in fact their fur can be black, brown, silver-blue, and occasionally, even white!

Black bears have small eyes, long noses, round ears, and a short tail. Their feet have strong, very curved claws for climbing, digging and tearing at their prey.

Black bears are excellent climbers. Sometimes they climb up to bald eagle nests to eat the eggs or chicks.

SNACK ON THIS!

A female black bear cub called Winnipeg, who lived in London Zoo from 1915 to 1934, was the inspiration for Winnie the Pooh.

Black bears spend most of their lives alone, unless they are females with cubs. Females give birth during winter hibernation, usually to two cubs.

American black bear facts

- **How heavy?** The average male weighs 300 lb.
- **How big?** 4-5 ft. tall
- **How fast?** Up to 35 mph

Black bear cubs stay with their mother until they are about two years old. After that, they go off to live alone.

More About American Black Bears

A bear snacks on some grass. Black bears eat up to 45 pounds a day before hibernation.

Black bears mostly eat nuts, fruits, and plants, but they also like to hunt. They prey on young deer, elk, and moose. Occasionally they might ambush a passing adult moose. They kill by biting the neck and shoulders or by using their paws to break the neck or back.

Black bears are not as aggressive as brown bears. They rarely attack humans, unless they are very hungry. Usually they will make mock charges, bare their teeth, and growl.

SNACK ON THIS!

The worst known black bear attack on humans occurred in May 1978 when a black bear killed three teenagers in Algonquin Park, Canada.

Like their brown bear cousins, black bears are good at fishing.

Black bears have been known to scavenge carcasses from cougars and wolverines. They sometimes even steal deer from human hunters. Occasionally they prey on domestic livestock, such as sheep, goats, calves, and pigs.

CHEW ON THAT!

Black bears can go without food for seven months during the winter.

Stealing human food is so much easier than hunting for the lazier black bears.

17

Polar Bear

The polar bear is a powerful, skilled, and patient hunter that roams the coastal regions of the Arctic. Unlike other bears, it eats almost only meat. Its main victims are ringed and bearded seals, young walruses, and the occasional beluga whale.

Polar bears travel an average of 9,000 miles a year in search of food.

SNACK ON THIS!

Believe it or not, polar bear fur isn't white, but transparent!

Polar bear facts

- **How heavy?** Males average 750-1,500 lb.
- **How big?** 8-10 ft.
- **How fast?** 3-6 mph in the water; 34 mph on land–faster than a reindeer!

Polar bears are perfectly adapted to their chilly environment. A four-inch layer of blubber and thick fur protects them from the cold. Their hollow outer hairs and black skin trap the sun's heat.

Polar bears have a number of advantages in the water. Their body fat gives them buoyancy and their broad forepaws, with webbed toes, make powerful paddles.

Polar bears are also the best swimmers in the bear family and can dive to a depth of 10 feet or more.

More About Polar Bears

A polar bear uses its nose to seek out its prey.

Polar bears are stealth hunters. Their victims rarely know what is happening until the attack is under way.

Blood marks the snow where a seal has recently been caught and killed by a polar bear.

They often ambush seals at their breathing holes. When the seal surfaces for air, the polar bear seizes it and crushes its skull with its teeth.

SNACK ON THIS!

Polar bears must kill 50 to 75 seals annually to survive.

Sometimes a polar bear might spot a seal on an ice floe. The bear creeps to within 40 feet of the seal, then suddenly charges forward to attack.

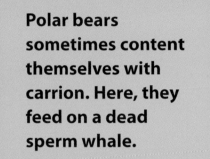

Polar bears sometimes content themselves with carrion. Here, they feed on a dead sperm whale.

Polar bears sometimes find seals' birthing dens beneath the ice. The bear rears onto its hind legs, then drops onto all fours, using its weight to smash through the ice and reach the baby seals.

Asian Black Bear

Asian black bears inhabit the mountain forests of South and East Asia. They are also known as moon bears because of the pale, crescent-shaped marking on their chests.

Asian black bears are loners. They can be aggressive, but generally prefer to avoid conflict.

Asian black bears are not fussy eaters. They will dine on insects, grubs, carrion, bees, eggs, fruit, plant matter, or food thrown out by humans.

SNACK ON THIS!

Naturalist Jim Corbett (1875–1955) once witnessed a fight between a huge black bear and a tiger. The bear eventually chased off the tiger, despite having half its nose and scalp torn off.

Fiercer than their American cousins, Asian black bears prey on mammals such as wild boar, water buffalo, sheep, or mountain goats. They kill them with powerful blows to the neck or back.

Leopards and tigers have occasionally had their kills stolen by Asian black bears.

CHEW ON THAT!

In the summer months, Asian black bears often build "nests" in trees. They sleep in them during the day and come down to feed at night.

Thanks to their strong, curved claws, Asian black bears are accomplished tree climbers.

Sloth Bear

Sloth bears are so named because scientists once thought they were sloths, not bears! Their slow, shuffling gait does appear slothful, but when alarmed they can move very fast indeed.

Sloth bears are expert termite hunters. They dig a hole in the top of a termite mound and stick their snouts in. Sloths have no front teeth, and their hairless, flexible lips form a tube through which the termites are sucked. The vacuuming sound can be heard up to 600 feet away!

The long, curved front claws of the sloth bear are ideal for digging up termite mounds.

SNACK ON THIS!

Baloo the friendly bear, from Rudyard Kipling's *Jungle Book*, was modeled on the sloth bear.

When threatened, sloth bears usually stand their ground, even against their most feared predator, the tiger. The bear will charge at the tiger, screaming. Most tigers will retreat at this point, as sloth bear claws can hurt!

Sloth bear facts

- **How heavy?** 180–310 lb.
- **How big?** 4.6–6.3 ft. in body length
- **Where?** The evergreen forests and grasslands of South Asia

A female sloth bear (right) threatens a male, exposing her flexible snout and missing front teeth.

Bengal tigers like to sneak up on sloth bears while they are busy feeding on termite mounds.

Sun Bear

The smallest of the great bears, the sun bear is found in the tropical rain forests of Southeast Asia. They live alone or in small groups.

The bear has sleek black fur and an orange-yellow crescent-shaped mark on its chest. Its large paws and long, curved, sharply pointed claws are ideal for tree climbing.

According to local legend, the sun bear's chest blaze represents the rising sun.

SNACK ON THIS!

Sun bears have loose neck skin, which allows them to turn around and bite animals that attack them from behind.

Sun bears are fierce animals with sharp teeth and powerful jaws. They enjoy dining on lizards, small birds, rodents, insects, fruit, eggs, and the young tips of palm trees.

Like many bears, the sun bear has a special fondness for honey. It uses its long, slender tongue, which measures up to 10 inches, to slurp up honey from beehives.

Sun bear facts

- **How heavy?** 65-110 lb.
- **How big?** 3.2-4.6 ft. in body length
- **Where?** Burma, Laos, Vietnam, Thailand, Malaysia, Sumatra, and Borneo

The sun bear is often called the dog bear by local people, and it's not hard to see why.

27

Giant Short-Faced Bear

Perhaps we can consider ourselves lucky that this monster no longer walks the Earth! The giant short-faced bear was the largest bear that ever lived and one of the biggest, most fearsome land predators of the Ice Age.

It inhabited the North American plains from about 1.3 million to 12,500 years ago and preyed on bison, deer, horses, and ground sloths.

The giant short-faced bear was about the height of a man when on all fours.

The bear had longer, more slender limbs than most modern bears.

Giant short-faced bear facts

- **How heavy?** 1,500 lb.
- **How tall?** 12 ft.
- **How fast?** Approx 30-45 mph

Exactly how this bear found food is a matter of debate. Although big, it had quite a slender build and may have struggled to bring down large animals.

A giant short-faced bear attacks a bison.

Some scientists believe it was very fast and could catch agile prey. Others say the bear was a "super-scavenger," using its enormous size to scare away smaller predators so it could steal their kills.

SNACK ON THIS!

The giant short-faced bear probably died out because of increased competition from brown bears entering North America from Asia—or maybe because it was hunted by early humans!

Glossary

ambush Launch a surprise attack from a concealed position.

beluga whale A small, white-toothed whale living in Arctic coastal waters.

blubber The fat of sea mammals such as whales and seals.

buoyancy The ability to float in water.

canine teeth Pointed teeth used by meat-eating mammals for piercing skin and tearing and ripping flesh.

carcass The dead body of an animal.

caribou A large North American reindeer.

carrion The decaying flesh of dead animals.

cougar A large American wild cat.

domestic livestock Tame animals, kept by farmers.

elk A large North American red deer.

forage Search for food.

formidable Inspiring fear or respect.

hibernation A period of sleep or rest that many animals undergo during the winter months.

ice floe A sheet of floating ice.

moose A large deer native to northern Eurasia and North America.

omnivore An animal that eats food of both plant and animal origin.

predator An animal that preys on other animals.

prey An animal that is hunted and killed by another animal for food.

rain forest A dense forest, rich in animal and plant life, usually found in tropical areas.

scavenge Search for and eat carrion or other discarded food.

sloth A slow-moving tropical American mammal.

stalk Pursue or approach stealthily.

termite A small, pale, soft-bodied insect that lives in large colonies, usually within a mound of earth.

wolverine A heavily built, short-legged meat-eating mammal with a shaggy dark coat and bushy tail.

Further information

Books

Bears by Jen Green (Amicus, 2011)

Black Bear: North America's Bear by Stephen R. Swinburne (Boyds Mill Press, 2009)

Face to Face with Polar Bears by Norbert Rosing (National Geographic, 2009)

Grizzly Bears by Jacqueline Dineen (Weigl, 2009)

Moon Bear by Brenda Z. Guiberson (Henry Holt, 2010)

Time for Kids: Bears! by Nicole Iorio (HarperCollins, 2005)

Web Sites

www.americanbear.org
The website of the American Bear Association is full of information about bears, including some great photos.

animals.howstuffworks.com/mammals/bear-info.htm
A comprehensive look at all things ursine (relating to bears).

www.bbc.co.uk/nature/family/Bear
Contains great video and sound clips of bears.

www.kidzone.ws/lw/bears/facts.htm
General and easily digestible information about bears of the world.

www.yourdiscovery.com/animalplanet/bears
Contains information about all the great bears, including their appearance, habitat, diet, and behavior.

Index

Page numbers in **bold** refer to pictures.